MW01289496

The Ultimate Beginner's Guide for Understanding Dogecoin and What You Need to Know

presentation of the information is without contract or any type of guarantee assurance.

The trademarks that are used are without any consent, and the publication of the trademark is without permission or backing by the trademark owner. All trademarks and brands within this book are for clarifying purposes only and are the owned by the owners themselves, not affiliated with this document.

Table Of Contents

Introduction

This book is for people who are interested in learning more about the Dogecoin currency and are not sure where to start or what information to rely on. I made this book in response to the high demand of people wanting to know more about Dogecoin and why there is so much hype around it.

The Internet today has many articles and misinformation about Dogecoin that confuse people who are interested in learning about this revolutionary cryptocurrency and possibly interested in purchasing some dogecoins themselves.

In this book, I am going to give you a short, concise guide for everything you need to know to get started with Dogecoin. The history of this currency as well as the current innovations that are going on in the Doigecoin market are key to understanding what the future will hold. We will also go over the different functions and options that a person has when it comes to purchasing their own dogecoins and how to use them.

And most importantly, we will go through the pros and cons of using Dogecoin so that you can understand everything you need to know before taking the plunge and investing in it yourself. Whether you plan on diversifying from Bitcoin, buying your first cryptocurrency in Dogecoin, or you just want to know more about why this trend is becoming so popular, it is important to know all the benefits and risks involved. This book also highlights Dogecoin's differences from other similar cryptocurrencies.

Cryptocurrency became popular in 2009 in the form of Bitcoin. Bitcoin was designed and developed to use a hybrid system of proof-of-stake and proof-of-work to address different vulnerabilities, such as mining monopoly and inflation. As cryptocurrency is being introduced to decentralize the production of money, Dogecoin is becoming one of the most prominent names in the cyptocurrency arena.

I recommend that you take notes while you are reading the book. This will ensure that you get the most out of the information in here. I want you to feel that you made a purchase that is worth your money and you can look over the notes of this book even after you've finished reading it. The notes will help you to pinpoint exactly what you need to implement and by writing things down, you will be able to recall specifics and how to handle certain situations when they arise.

Lastly, remember that everything in this book has been compiled through research, my own experiences, as well as the experiences of others, so feel free to question what you have read in this book. I encourage you to do your own research on the things that you want to look deeper into. The more you understand about Dogecoin, the more educated your decision-making process will be when it comes to purchasing and transacting your own, or giving advice   to   others.

Chapter 1:

It Started with a Doge

Whether it is for entertainment, academics or work, the presence of the internet can be felt in every part of society. Today, students are able to log in at home for their lessons and homework and with one click, all the information they need will appear before them. Businessmen are able to communicate with their counterparts in other continents. A single homemade video can be seen by thousands in just one day and with millions of purchases and exchanges being done online today, it was only a matter of time before online currencies joined in on the fray.

One of the by-products of the Digital Age's onslaught in society is cryptocurrency. Cryptocurrency, or digital currency, is based on cryptographs rather than actual trust. The production of cryptocurrency is limited, and any cryptocurrency system cannot produce excessively. Individuals can procure cryptocurrency through mining or the process of solving algorithms to gain digital currency.

With actual money, governing bodies and even individuals are able to influence its production. The same cannot be said with cryptocurrencies, however. As such, there is no governing body that regulates cryptocurrencies. Instead, cryptocurrencies follow a mathematical system that was created by the currency's original creator.

In this recent explosion of new cryptocurrencies, there have been many that have sprung up, such as Bitcoin, Litecoin, Peercoin, and Namecoin. Most of the time, these currencies can only be exchanged with each other and not with actual fiat currency. Even so, their usage has been gaining a steady stream of followers, for a variety of reasons, ranging from convenience to safety.

Surprisingly, one of the most popular cryptocurrencies today is based on a joke - meme, to be more precise. Dogecoins are based on memes that feature Shibe Inus dogs with various texts using the Comic sans font. The texts imply the thoughts running through the dog's head and the internet world has christened these memes as Doge.

Originally, these memes came from the site, Homestar Runner, which featured a short video. The video contained a puppet misspelling the word "Dog" as "Doge". Eventually, the meme was developed through different channels such as Reddit and Tumblr. The Meme of the Year 2013 winner is the origin, as well as the mascot, of the now-famous Dogecoins.

Jackson Palmer, who is part of Adobe's marketing department in Australia and was an avid follower of the development of cryptocurrencies, started Dogecoins' journey, with a post on the social media website Twitter stating, "Investing in Dogecoin, pretty sure it's the next big thing."

That statement garnered numerous replies, all urging Palmer to pursue the project. Palmer bought the domain Dogecoin.com and designed it with the Doge as the main logo. Still, he had yet to have the system to fully launch Dogecoin as an actual digital currency.

Meanwhile, on the other side of the world, Billy Markus was also attempting to create his own cryptocurrency. The Portland-based programmer was already developing a coin that he entitled "Bells," when he saw a link in the IRC Chat Room for Dogecoin.com and immediately became interested. He reached out to Palmer and together, they formed Dogecoin. It was then launched on December 8th, 2013. According to Palmer, "It's important to note that this wasn't some master plan, it was just the two of us throwing a few emails back and forth before we pushed it out there."

Chapter 2:

The Rise and Development of Dogecoin

The foundations of Dogecoin can be traced all the way back to the Bitcoin, which source code is open to the public. Billy Markus' basis was the Luckycoin (LKY), a cryptocurrency that uses a peer-to-peer network. Operated by the Luckycoin Foundation, Luckycoin serves as a casino coin for miners, where a random reward was given out whenever a block was mined.

Meanwhile, the Luckycoin and in turn, Dogecoin, was also based on another cryptocurrency, the Litecoin. The latter has its roots set from Bitcoin and was essentially created to address certain issues of the said cryptocurrency. The popularity of Bitcoin gave way to problems with transaction speed.

Ultimately, Bitcoin's block chain, or its transaction record, became so severely overworked that it duplicated. Confusion erupted as there were two Bitcoins to contend with. The issue was only resolved when one of the two block chains became more updated than the other, confirming that it was indeed the true Bitcoin.

Frequently, more merchants require large numbers of transactions with small values. Unfortunately, Bitcoin is more used in larger values, which takes up more time. Litecoin, which was launched by Ryan Rohypol on October 7th, 2011 via GitHub, cut down Bitcoin's transaction speed. Transactions with smaller values were made possible due to Litecoin's having more coins in circulation. In fact, it had four times more coins than Bitcoin. Thus, while Bitcoin had a record of 10 minutes per transaction, Litecoin was able to conduct a transaction in only 2.5 minutes.

One of Litecoin's primary characteristics is also the use of Scrypt, as opposed to Bitcoin's SHA256d. This makes Bitcoin-mining equipment virtually ineffective against Litecoin. This also allows Litecoin to be able to withstand users with more powerful hardware.

From Litecoin, Dogecoin has adapted Scrypt, as well as its faster transaction speed. Luckycoin provides its reward aspect and its template for the Dogewallet. One of its most popular features, however, is its Tipping Bot. "Tipping" refers to the act of giving Dogecoins to other users for various reasons. Users have been known to tip others when they've uploaded a great picture, done a good deed, and so on.

Dogecoin has initially set its production target to 100 billion Dogecoins. Although Jackson Palmer and Billy Markus created it, the whole system is now being regulated and run by its ever-growing network.

Despite it's funny origins, the success of Dogecoin is undeniable. On December 13th, 2013, just a few days after its launch, Dogecoin made an unprecedented 300% jump in just 24 hours. It went from a Wednesday value of $0.00026 to a Thursday value of $0.00095. This placed Dogecoin in the Top Ten Digital Currencies of today. This is especially impressive considering that in the same period, Bitcoin and other cryptocurrencies' values crashed because the People's Bank of China had decided to no longer accept Bitcoins.

The cryptocurrency giant's value at the time went down by 50%, while Dogecoin continued its massive climb to reach up to 360%. Dogecoin has even overtaken Bitcoin and other cryptocurrencies in transaction count.

If that wasn't enough, Cryptsy joined COINS-E and Coined Up in permitting Dogecoin in their exchanges. This event has reportedly increased Dogecoin's value up to four times.

At that time, the total market value of the Dogecoin reached $60 million. However, that was not the only major statistic that grew. Its circle of followers has also widened dramatically. Businessmen, entrepreneurs, students and many other individuals now make up the Dogecoin community. This community has even garnered many notable achievements in such a short time, considering that they've just started.

One of these achievements was the collection of 27 million Dogecoins - which is worth roughly $30,000.00 - for the Jamaican Bobsled Team. The team needed funds to be able to join the Sochi Winter Olympic Games in Russia. This incident caused the Bitcoin-Dogecoin exchange rate to drop by 50%. Afterward, the Dogecoin community also supported Shiva Keshavan, the first Indian to participate in Luge at the Winter Olympics.

Another notable occurrence was when Dogecoin suffered its first hacking incident on Christmas day. A hacker was able to steal around $12,000 worth of Dogecoins from different users by entering the Dogecoin system and tweaking the send and receive function to wire coins to a particular address. Dogecoin.com released a statement in their forums, saying that upon looking at their log record, they were able to discover several attempts of hacking and that they would refund the lost Dogecoins to their respective users.

Even with this proclamation, the Dogecoin community still came together and formed SaveDogemas. Here, they worked to return what the hacker took. They would go on to raise over 11 million Dogecoins. Jackson Palmer was even able to set up the Dogecoin Foundation, a non-profit organization that is, "for the purpose of spreading the use of the currency through goodwill and charitable endeavors." Some of its more successful initiatives are Doge4water and Doge4kids. They are also aiding several charities such as The League against Aids and Shiba Scout Rescue.

There are many more tidbits and highlights that this quirky currency has collected. There is the Chinese investor who bought $5 million worth of Dogecoins, the Subaru Impreza that sold for 7.5 million Dogecoins, and there are even baristas out there accepting Dogecoins for coffee.

The rise of Dogecoins has indeed been phenomenal. It is even said that the Dogecoin's first 100 days is better than the original cryptocurrency's first 1,000. It is still a young endeavor, yet its achievements have been massive. Even its creators, Markus and Palmer, are amazed at the heights their project has achieved in such little time. Many look forward to what else this "joke" can turn into.

Chapter 2:

The Altcoins

Alternative coins or Altcoin is another term used for cryptocurrencies like Dogecoin. They are classified as such because most of them followed in the footsteps of Bitcoin. With the popularity of virtual currencies growing, the birth of other competitors cannot be stopped. Different groups and individuals have also tried their hand in this digital trade, resulting in the beginnings of a dynamic digital economy.

Slowly, but surely, the digital world is resembling reality in more ways than one. It is important to know what other altcoins are out there. They will surely affect the development of not only Dogecoin, but the whole internet currency system, as well. The previous chapters have already discussed Bitcoin, the massive cryptocurrency. Most altcoins, like Litecoin and Dogecoin, have taken their foundations from this. This is mostly due to the fact that its source code is open to the public.

One of the Bitcoin look-alikes is the Peercoin. To accumulate Peercoins, one must mine algorithms, similar to the process of mining Bitcoins. Unlike Bitcoin, however, Peercoins have an unlimited mining capacity. There are plans to introduce a 1% inflation rate to Peercoins, which could be a beneficial thing because it will likely make Peercoins last longer in the market. Peercoins are also set to move from Bitcoin's proof-of-work mining process to its own proof-of-stake process.

Rather than relying heavily on processing power, Peercoin will be depending on the amount of stock a user owns. The percentage of Peercoin stock that users have will translate into the amount of blocks that they will be able to mine. Also, this altcoin is about to launch the concept of "Age" for its coins. Basically, stagnancy will cause coins to age, but if spent or traded, coin age will be brought back to its original form.

Meanwhile, Primecoin focuses on science. This is the first of its kind, where mining coins will actually benefit society by contributing scientific knowledge. With Primecoin, miners search for prime numbers and new blocks are created every minute. Obviously, this will mean faster transactions. Block rewards are also determined by the level of difficulty the miner encounters. The intentions of Primecoin are good, but they do cause several problems. The biggest one is the instability of supply and demand.

As Primecoin attracts more miners, difficulty levels are sure to increase, which will result in a lower production of coins. Instead of creating more coins to satisfy the demand, supply lessens. Economically speaking, this is the opposite of the desired goal. Also, prices will frequently rise and fall. Instability in that score is another reason that miners may stay away.

Namecoin is another altcoin that has risen in the ranks. Its uses go beyond that of a normal digital currency. It is not limited to payments alone. Although it does adapt many of Bitcoin's principles, it is also able to create a decentralized Domain Name System (DNS). With ".bit" as its top-level domain, users are able to oversee emails, source websites, and retrieve IP addresses. Still, it maintains its currency function and users are able to check both Bitcoin and Namecoin block chains simultaneously when mining.

Probably the most unique altcoin out there today is Ripple. It is not a copy or even a direct competitor of Bitcoin. Instead, it is establishing itself as a channel for payment and exchange. It is not competing against Bitcoin or the other cryptocurrencies. Alternatively, Ripple wishes to act as a support platform. Ripple still has its own currency, which are called Ripples, but its focus is more on its payment and exchange network. Users are able to send and receive money, whether it is actual dollars or cryptocurrency.

Ripple is especially attractive to users as it charges no transaction fees. It also enables people to interact directly with the market, instead of having to use third-party intermediaries to do their transactions for them. Again, this will result in less fees and faster transactions. Ripple also makes it possible to trade between exchanges through the issuance of IOUs. IOUs can be traded from exchange to exchange.

Ripple does not use mining to generate coins, but there has recently been a program introduced where one is given free Ripples for any computer power donation. Ripple has been causing ripples (pun intended) across the cryptocurrency field. Even big companies like Google Ventures and Lightspeed Venture have taken notice. They, as well as many others, have provided capital for the altcoin.

One of the most similar altcoins to Dogecoin is the Fedoracoin. It capitalizes in its tipping function, which makes its social network extremely important to its success, since it will need generous users with coins to spare. Still, it is not a total copycat, it does have innovations of its own.

One of these innovations is the "coin mixer." The pioneer of this innovation, Fedoracoin includes the coin mixer in the wallets so that users will have anonymous transactions. This altcoin has also created tools that allow users to make easier transaction payments from their own websites.

The alternative coins mentioned above are just the tip of the proverbial iceberg. Many more are appearing everywhere. An Internet search for these terms will result in hundreds of pages. Worldcoin, Feathercoin, Anoncoin, Protoshares, Devcoin, and Earthcoin, are just a few that one will find.

At the end of the day, Dogecoin is only one of many in this field. Yet, it seems to be the one enjoying the most success in such a short period of time. Looking at the above information, it has a lot of similarities with the other cryptocurrencies. Like most of them, its roots came from Bitcoin. So what have Jack Palmer and Markus Jackson done differently to create such a passionate following?

Marketing is the answer. Apparently, having a dog as one's main logo appeals to hordes of users. It speaks of the accessibility of the coin and it also lends it a kind of identity. It is probably one of the only altcoins out there that looks like it is having fun, whereas other coins look too serious. The history of other cryptocurrencies with shady exploits may also be a factor, as Dogecoin is still relatively new to the field.

Bitcoin's history with hackers, theft, and even drugs, has caused some users to be turned off from any activity with cryptocurrencies. Impressively, Dogecoin is managing to remove the intimidating aura of digital currencies. Memes, after all, do not usually intimidate. They make people laugh and they make people interested, which is why more users are attracted to Dogecoin. Not only does it draw altcoin veterans to its fold, it also enables newcomers to try it out.

People who usually hesitate in joining the digital currency party find encouragement because Dogecoin makes it so easy. What Dogecoin is saying is: You don't need to be a financial expert to be a part of Dogecoin. This message has allowed the circle for cryptocurrency enthusiasts to widen considerably.

The most difficult obstacle that cryptocurrencies face is making people truly understand what it is. People hardly know how these currencies work and how it can benefit their lives. That is why Dogecoin is creating waves in its field. As Markus puts it, "In hindsight, it was obvious that cryptocurrency was ready for something that was more accessible, and a meme is obviously accessible. Everyone recognizes the doge meme. It's based on a dog, and everyone loves dogs. It was a perfect storm."

That is not to say that Dogecoins and other cryptocurrencies have no disadvantages. They do have several. One of them is that cryptocurrencies are not physical currencies that we can hold or trade. You cannot use them to buy goods at your grocery store, at least not yet. There are, of course, some exceptions to that rule. But as of the current moment, this is the status quo.

There is also the issue of value fluctuation. Cryptocurrencies have not yet established themselves firmly enough to have price stability. Even Bitcoin is still having a hard time maintaining its swinging price. Dogecoins are on a high right now. However, it has taken a fall before and no one can say that it will not happen again. Also, if its own economy is unstable, Dogecoins will surely be affected by it. For any merchant, it is frustrating to have to adhere to constantly changing prices.

Meanwhile, the dependency of virtual currencies on technology can be a double-edged sword. On one hand, transactions are easier and faster with technology. There will no longer be a need to join long bank lines and there will be no more hassle of carrying around cash.

Transactions can be done anytime, not just during an institution's operating hours. On the other hand, this will also make a user's money susceptible to technological glitches. Computer and hard drive crashes, and even viruses, can cause anyone to lose access to their wallets.

As it is still a fairly new system, virtual currencies still have a lot to go through and many mistakes to make. They have not yet been perfected, which makes its youth one of its biggest disadvantages of all. This is also one of the reasons for others to be wary of it.

Still, even though it is at the early part of its development, the advantages of cryptocurrency are already prominent. One of its strongest benefits is that it is not limited to one country alone. Governments set boundaries for real currencies. While cryptocurrency is not surrounded by exchange rates, country transaction fees, taxes and other international legalities, the use of digital coins in the international sense are faster and have less problematic pathways.

One advantage that is always emphasized is the anonymity involved in using virtual currency. This is very important in today's generation as people are now having a hard time with privacy. Most financial transactions have a way of providing a home address, phone number and other information that most people are not comfortable in sharing. Cryptocurrencies hold no personal information and for most people, this is a huge selling point.

In joining Dogecoin or any other cryptocurrency, the pros and cons must always be weighed. Some will feel that the advantages do outstrip the disadvantages that come with this new wave. However, all investments, not just cryptocurrency, always involve risks. There is something to be said, however, for cryptocurrency has the potential to turn a small investment into a huge pay off in so little time. Dogecoin is proof of that.

Chapter 4:

To The Moon

As mentioned in the previous chapter, Dogecoin is one of the easiest and most accessible forms of cryptocurrency. For any beginner in virtual currency, this is probably the best place to start. The set up is easy and there is no need to study big books in finance and computer technology to be able to grasp it.

The Dogecoin client, Dogecoin-qt, is available on Dogecoin.com to download. Once downloaded, the file dogecoin-qt is where you will need to start. The interface of Dogecoin retains the personality of its mascot. It still contains its fun identity with tabs stating Wow, Pls Send, Much Receive, Many History, Very Address, and Dig. These are in place of Bitcoin and Litecoin's Overview, Send, Receive, Transactions, and

Addresses tabs, respectively. The command Dig is for Dogecoin's mining function.

It is important to secure the Dogewallet during set up. Although Dogecoin is secure, it is still safer to be able to save it in a hard drive or any other memory device. To do so, the settings tab must be accessed and the Encrypt Wallet command must be clicked. Passwords should be remembered or kept somewhere safe; otherwise, accumulated coins can be lost forever.

Dogecoins can be obtained through numerous sources. Again, there is the tipping bot, where one can receive tips in dogecoins for posting entertaining content. Dogecoin Faucets are also readily available. These are websites like Dogefaucet.com and InDogeWeTrust.com that regularly give out Dogecoins. In fact, there are many other subreddits that aid Dogecoin beggars. Finally, Dogecoin's three exchanges, namely, Cryptsy, Coins-E, and CoinedUp, are available for trading Dogecoin.

The ease of the Dogecoin set up is one of its many attractions. It is no wonder that this cryptocurrency is currently rising up the ranks of the best virtual currencies out there. Dogecoin, along with Litecoin, Namecoin, Feathercoin, and Peercoin, is one of the altcoins selected by AltQuick.co. This is a platform for cryptocurrency and USD exchanges.

This is a pretty big deal in the Dogecoin community, or in any cryptocurrency community, for that matter. There has always been a scarcity of Crypto-USD exchanges, even for the more established cryptocurrencies, like Litecoin. To be included in AltQuick.co speaks volumes of the demand for Dogecoin.

Meanwhile, even the enthusiasm for the meme altcoin has spread far and wide. It has jumped out of the virtual world and is even expressing itself in other ways. In Vancouver, a Dogecoin ATM was installed as the CoinFest Digital Currency Festival was being held. A Nexus 7 tablet, a briefcase, and a money validator made up this homemade ATM machine. It's not that high-tech but the ingenuity is marvelous. Users are able to buy dogecoins just by pressing a few buttons and inserting cash.

Vancouver's makeshift ATM is just the beginning. On March 22nd, 2014, in the BIT Center in Tijuana, two ATMs were installed that would buy and sell three cryptocurrencies: Bitcoin, Litecoin, and Dogecoin. One ATM is said to accept United States Dollars, while the other will be taking Mexican Pesos.

Moving along to Asia, Dogecoin has been recently added to two new exchanges. The first is to BTC38, a Chinese Exchange, and ANX, an exchange from Hongkong. These occurences caused Dogecoin's market cap to rise above $90 million.

The future seems very bright for the cryptocurrency. Still, not everybody feels confident in the future of Dogecoin. There are those who say that the Dogecoin will die, as any fad will soon enough. Others cite its lack of innovative ventures to be a dangerous sign. There are also groups who cling to its survival, believing that the Dogecoin is more than a trendy commodity.

When asked, Dogecoin's creators also have several things to say. For Jackson Palmer, tipping is the way to continue Dogecoin's journey. He believes that the results of the tipping bot, as seen on Reddit, is evidence in itself. At 7,200 tippers a week, this is a good argument. Palmer also predicts that the Dogecoin community will play a huge part in the future of the altcoin. The community's nature is very giving and he thinks that this will carry on and continue to fuel each other's success. Ultimately, an overall adoption of cryptocurrencies was what he had always envisioned.

Meanwhile, a recent decision by Palmer and Markus has given way to even more speculation of their altcoin's future. It was Palmer who announced that Dogecoin would have a limited inflation each year. Bitcoins and many other altcoins have a limited number of coins to produce, attesting to their deflationary nature.

In Palmer's statement, he said that once production has reached its original limit of 100 billion coins, rewards will continue at 10k per block. Angry users complained that the decision would decrease the value of Dogecoins over time, instead of the opposite.

After all, once the demand increases and the supply dwindles, early buyers of Dogecoins would see their investment's value soar higher than ever. There are also those who support the decision, economists among them. They view the inflation rate as a chance for Dogecoins to extend its usefulness and become much more than a passing venture.

The Dogecoin has yet to reach its first full year, but so far, it has been eventful. The Shiba dog, which first entertained the world with its amusing thoughts and musings, is now providing even more value with the heights its currency is reaching.

The fact that it started as a joke is what makes it even more impressive. For its creators, they believe that the biggest contribution that Dogecoin has provided is the awareness that it has created in society for cryptocurrencies. It has made itself known among neophytes. They creators have been able to get people to start mining and form the communities that were supportive of their Doge. In fact, even after incidents like value crashes and hacking, their followers are still saying their favorite catchphrase. They are still going "to the moon."

Dogecoins have little value in themselves. Like all cryptocurrencies, it cannot be treated like real fiat money just yet. However, with the way

Dogecoin is rapidly expanding, this may not be the case in the near future. Transactions in every day life are becoming less about physical cash and moving more towards electronic payment.

As a matter of fact, there have already been several episodes of Dogecoin transactions outside of the virtual world. There are now numerous online companies and businesses accepting Dogecoins. Hand crafted infinity scarves, beef jerkies and graphic design services are just some of the things that Dogecoins can now acquire. Even Palmer's wish to be able to buy a soda using cryptocurrency may be right around the corner. A Bit Bourbon Steamed Burger Stand has sprung up in East London, one of the first places in Britain to accept Dogecoins.

When asked, owner, Rynkiewicz, believes that these coins will be the future, though it will not necessarily replace normal fiat currency. A lot of charities and fund-raisers are also receiving Dogecoins, granting Billy Markus' own desire for altcoins to have a useful contribution to society.

The future seems very bright for the months-old cryptocurrency. The leaps and bounds it has taken is a testament to how fast technology can bring change in a current market. In a matter of months, an innocent Shibe dog was transformed into one of the most used and talked about virtual currencies today. It is amazing how a random idea, conceived with a bottle of beer in hand, can go so far.

Conclusion

I hope this book was able to help you to learn about the basics of Dogecoin, the different options you have, and how the future looks for this new currency. Now that you have learned the important factors about Dogecoin, you can finally decide if you want to take the plunge, or if you can recommend it to your family and friends.

Plus, a little addition to your knowledge doesn't really hurt, right? It's good to know about new innovations because it keeps us in the know and up-to-date in a world where every big city has meet-up groups dedicated to learning more about cryptocurrencies.

Thanks again and good luck to you in your journey if you decide to get involved with cryptocurrency!

Made in the USA
Columbia, SC
01 February 2021

32002314R00026